READING EXERCISES
Second Edition

READ BEYOND

the

LINES

Book C

by
Arthur I. Gates and Celeste Comegys Peardon
revised by
Betty I. LaClair

TEACHERS COLLEGE PRESS

Teachers College, Columbia University
New York and London   1982

Published by Teachers College Press, 1234 Amsterdam Avenue, New York, NY 10027
Copyright © 1963, 1982 by Teachers College, Columbia University

ISBN 0-8077-5989-9

Manufactured in the United States of America

87 86 85 84 83 82   1 2 3 4 5 6

Illustrations by Ner Beck

ACKNOWLEDGMENTS

The authors and Teachers College Press extend thanks to those whose interest, cooperation, and permission to reprint have made possible the preparation of *Reading Exercises, Second Edition*. All possible care has been taken to trace the ownership of selections from other copyrighted sources and to make full acknowledgment for their use.

Acknowledgment for permission to use copyrighted material in this book and to make specified abridgments or adaptations is made to these authors and publishers:

Ex. 2. "The Old Woman and the Physician," from *A Harvest of World Folk Tales* edited by Milton Rugoff. Copyright 1949 by The Viking Press, Inc. © renewed 1977 by Milton Rugoff. Reprinted by permission of Viking Penguin Inc.

Ex. 19. "Crime, Cops, Computers," by W. David Malcolm, Jr., from *The Best of Creative Computing*, D. H. Ahl, ed., 1976. Reprinted by permission of Creative Computing Press.

Exs. 20, 21. "Test Yourself," reprinted by permission of G. P. Putnam's Sons from *Jokes & How to Tell Them* by Sonny Fox and Robert Gray. Copyright © 1965 by Sonny Fox and Robert Gray.

Ex. 24. "Cases of Accidental Reporting," reprinted with permission from the 1980 edition of *The Old Farmer's Almanac* published by Yankee, Inc., Dublin, N.H.

TO THE STUDENT

To be a good reader, you must be able to read in different ways, for different reasons. In this book you will practice getting facts and meanings that are not directly stated in what you read. The answers to questions are not there in *words,* but the *idea* is there.

Most of the exercises are like the first one: there is a story to read, and on the back of the story page are questions about the story. *Think* about the story as you read it; then answer the questions. Choose the best answer for each question, and circle the letter in front of it. Sometimes the question is really a sentence with the last part missing, and the correct answer is the missing part. If you aren't sure which answer is correct, look back at the story and find the clues you need to figure it out.

A few of the exercises do not have questions. Instead, there are blanks in the story, and you will write the words that make sense in the blanks. Exercise 6 is the first one like this.

Don't be afraid to ask questions while you are working.

If you are going to check your own answers after you finish each exercise, you will use the Answer Page. And you can keep track of your scores on the Progress Chart.

If you need help with the first exercise, or with the Answer Page or the Progress Chart, ask your teacher.

One Sunday at the beginning of the hunting season, my uncle Dan came up to hunt deer on our farm in Vermont. Some friends of his were to arrive by car on Tuesday.

Uncle Dan was already well acquainted with many of the animals on the farm. He carried milk to the barn cats, saved our dog from a porcupine, and rid the place of a couple of woodchucks. Our canary sang whenever Uncle Dan came into the kitchen. But he had not yet met our new pet, Princess, although we had told him about her.

Late Tuesday afternoon, just before his friends arrived, Uncle Dan shouldered his gun and started across the south pasture. Behind him, and unseen by him, Princess trotted softly, wearing a red ribbon around her neck.

Uncle Dan's friends drove up the hill just in time to see a hilarious sight. Crossing the pasture was their friend, Dan the deer-stalker, carrying his gun. And tripping daintily along behind him was a little deer!

1. What is this story mainly about?
   a. work that is done on a farm
   b. Uncle Dan's friends
   c. a funny thing that happened in Vermont

2. Princess was following Uncle Dan because _____.
   a. she was a hunting dog
   b. she liked people
   c. she thought he was a robber

3. Why were Uncle Dan's friends coming to Vermont?
   a. to see Uncle Dan
   b. to go hunting
   c. to see a princess

4. Which sentence below is not directly stated in the story but seems to be true?
   a. Uncle Dan was already well acquainted with the animals on the farm.
   b. Uncle Dan arrived after his friends did.
   c. It is very unusual to see a deer following a hunter.

5. Which word best describes the deer episode in this story?
   a. amusing
   b. frightening
   c. serious

6. What do you think Uncle Dan did when he finally looked behind him?
   a. He shot the deer.
   b. He ran away.
   c. He laughed.

4

2

An old woman, who had become blind, called in a physician. She promised him, before witnesses, that if he would restore her eyesight she would give him a most handsome reward. However, if he did not cure her and her malady remained, he would receive nothing.

The agreement was concluded, and the physician tampered from time to time with the old woman's eyes. Meanwhile, bit by bit, he carried off her goods.

After a time, he set about the task in earnest and cured her. But the old woman, on recovering her sight, saw none of her goods left in the house. When, therefore, the physician asked her for payment, she continually put him off with excuses. He summoned her at last before the judges.

"What this man says is true enough," she said to the judges. "I promised to give him his fee if my sight was restored, and nothing if my malady remained. Now, then, he says that I am cured. But I say just the contrary, for when my malady first came on, I could see all sorts of furniture and goods in my house; but now, when he says he has restored my sight, I cannot see a single bit of either."

Adapted from A Harvest of World Folk Tales

1. What is this folk tale about?
   a. an old physician who became blind
   b. an old woman who got even
   c. a blind woman who was not cured

2. Which word best describes the actions of the old woman?
   a. clever
   b. malicious
   c. kind

3. The physician was _____.
   a. handsome
   b. contrary
   c. dishonest

4. What did the old woman mean when she spoke of her "malady"?
   a. a ringing in her ears
   b. her blindness
   c. her furniture

5. If you were the judge, how would you resolve this case?
   a. Dismiss the case for lack of evidence.
   b. Rule that the old woman should pay the physician as soon as her furniture and goods were returned.
   c. Send the old woman to prison.

6. Choose the best title for this story.
   a. An Old Woman
   b. A Handsome Reward
   c. To Catch a Thief

The motor purred smoothly as the boat sped through the water to the fishing spot. Fred and his two brothers had discovered this spot a few days earlier in the marshes.

Eagerly the young fishermen baited their hooks. They waited, but the fish were not biting. After a long afternoon, the sun went behind the clouds and big drops of rain splashed into the water. Still no fish! The brothers decided to head for home.

When they were almost in sight of their own dock, the motor stalled. All their efforts to start it again failed. With a broken oar and one of Fred's shoes, they tried to row. But now the tide had changed and a strong wind sprang up. Their boat was driven back into the marshes.

The boys anchored the boat securely. Luckily, they were warmly dressed; but they had no lights and no food. During the night they saw the lights of three rescue boats. They shouted themselves hoarse, but no one heard them.

Daylight came at last. Just after daybreak a Coast Guard boat picked up the three tired, hungry boys and delivered them to their own dock. They had no fish to show, but they certainly had a story to tell!

1. This story tells _____.
   a. why a motor stalled when boys went fishing
   b. how some boys repaired the motor of their boat
   c. what happened when three boys went fishing

2. The first rescue attempt was made _____.
   a. just after daybreak
   b. when the rain began
   c. during the night

3. Which word best describes how the boys must have felt when they could not make themselves heard by the rescue boats?
   a. miserable
   b. excited
   c. angry

4. Which sentence below is not directly stated in the story but seems to be true?
   a. The story of the missing boys was on the radio.
   b. The concerned parents called the Coast Guard for help.
   c. The boys slept all night in the boat.

5. What did the boys probably do after they were rescued?
   a. went to school
   b. went fishing
   c. ate a hearty breakfast

6. Choose the best title for this story.
   a. A Rainy Evening
   b. An All-Night Fishing Trip
   c. The Heroic Coast Guard

PERFECT SCORE: 6   YOUR SCORE: _____

4

"Break, one nine! Break, one nine!"

Now Channel 19 was cleared for use.

"Yellow Bird please copy: down four-wheeler on Route 20 north, 84 mile marker," came the trucker's voice on the CB radio.

The response was immediate. "Thanks, Good Buddy, I'll get on it right away. What's your handle?"

Again the trucker's voice: "Coffeeman."

"OK, Coffeeman, catch you later."

The girl reached for the phone, dialed the police, and made the report of the stalled car on Route 20 north.

For five years Yellow Bird had been keeping an eye on traffic with her home-based citizens-band radio. All the truckers who passed through her area knew Yellow Bird's voice and admired her for the service she provided for motorists in trouble. But there was one thing the truckers didn't know. Yellow Bird made those phone calls from a wheelchair because a traffic accident five years earlier had deprived her of the use of her legs.

1. Why did the trucker say "Break, one nine"?
   a. to report a broken radio connection
   b. to call one of his buddies on Route 19
   c. to indicate that he wanted to use Channel 19

2. What does "down four-wheeler" mean?
   a. a car in trouble
   b. down the four-lane highway
   c. a four-car accident

3. Why were the police called?
   a. to report a stolen car
   b. to get help for a car with engine trouble
   c. to report a reckless driver

4. What does "keeping an eye on traffic" mean in this story?
   a. watching the traffic from a window
   b. reading about traffic accidents in the paper
   c. listening for traffic reports on a CB radio

5. Which sentence below is not directly stated in the story but seems to be true?
   a. Yellow Bird wanted to be useful.
   b. Yellow Bird had once worked as a trucker.
   c. Yellow Bird was the victim of a traffic accident.

6. What was Yellow Bird's real name?
   a. "Good Buddy"
   b. "Canary"
   c. The story doesn't say.

7. Yellow Bird called the trucker "Good Buddy" because _____.
   a. that was his special CB name
   b. that is what CB users often call each other
   c. that was his real name

10

On the front of the General Post Office building in New York City, these words are cut into the stone: "Neither snow, nor rain, nor heat, nor gloom of night stays these couriers from the swift completion of their appointed rounds." This quotation is from Herodotus, a Greek historian who lived nearly 2,500 years ago. He was talking about the postal system of the ancient Persians.

When we think today of swift mail delivery, we think of trains, trucks, and airplanes. But other means are also used to get the mail through. In some country districts where roads are steep and rough, horses still travel the mail routes as in the old days of the Pony Express. On the narrow trails leading down into the Grand Canyon, mail is carried by sure-footed mules. Dog sleds loaded with bags of letters and packages are still common in Alaska. No matter how isolated the area may be, some courier on his appointed round will carry your letter. Of course it may be delayed, for a while, by a postal strike. But neither snow, nor rain, nor heat, nor gloom of night will stop its relatively swift delivery!

1. What does this story describe?
   a. mail delivery long ago
   b. present-day means used to deliver mail
   c. the postal system in ancient Persia

2. What does the quotation on the New York General Post Office mean?
   a. No matter what the weather is like, the mail will be delivered.
   b. Postmen should not go on strike.
   c. Postmen must be swift runners.

3. Which means of delivering mail would be considered old-fashioned today?
   a. delivery by trucks and trains
   b. delivery by airplane
   c. delivery by horse, mule, and dog sled

4. Which statement below is true?
   a. You always receive mail within forty-eight hours.
   b. You can receive mail no matter where you live.
   c. You can receive mail only if there is a post office less than ten miles away.

5. What do you think was the author's main purpose in writing this story?
   a. to criticize
   b. to give praise
   c. to give information

6. Choose the best title for this story.
   a. Swift Couriers from Persia
   b. Living Up to an Old Motto
   c. Fast Mail by Airplane

PERFECT SCORE: 6   YOUR SCORE: _____

When you are reading, what do you do when you come to a word you don't know? Do you ever just try to read the rest of the sentence to see if you can understand it *without* that word? Very often, the clues you get by reading more of a story will help you to know what a word is.

In this exercise, and in three more to come later in the book, you will practice this kind of reading. In these exercises, words have been left out of many sentences. Can you guess what the missing words are by reading the rest of the sentence—or the sentence before, or the next sentence, or the rest of the paragraph? Write the missing words in the blanks. Do the sentences make sense now?

Don't worry if you are not sure about the correct spelling of a word. Either look it up in the dictionary or spell it the way it sounds. But write or print neatly, so your teacher can tell what word you mean.

The first two blanks in this story have been filled in for you. Now read the story and fill in the other missing words.

• • •

Dreams can come true—and boys and girls sometimes do get lucky breaks! A little more than a hundred years ago, a boy's _____lucky_____ break was the chance to learn
                          1
_____how_____ to send messages over the telegraph wires.
     2
Young Tom didn't have anyone to teach him that. He didn't go to _____; he was educated at home. But even
                3
if he had been in school, his teachers wouldn't have

_____ him about telegraphy. The only sending
      4
key was at the railroad _____.
                              5

13

One morning Tom was at the station selling newspapers. He was on the platform talking with the telegraph agent when _____ noticed the agent's small son playing on the tracks. Suddenly a freight _____ began backing into the station. Just _____ time Tom grabbed the child! The train knocked _____ both over, but the little boy _____ safe in Tom's arms.

The grateful father wanted _____ reward Tom. So Tom asked for the one thing he wanted most, from the one person who could _____ it to him. He asked to _____ taught to send messages _____ the telegraph wires. Of course, the agent agreed to teach him.

That was Thomas Edison's lucky break!

14

Every spring, millions of salmon leave the Pacific Ocean and swim many miles upstream to lay their eggs in the quiet, shallow waters of the upper Columbia River. No matter how difficult the journey, the salmon persist in going. They may travel ten to twenty miles a day. They swim against the current, often battling swift rapids. They jump waterfalls ten feet high. But when Bonneville Dam was built, it formed a barrier 197 feet high; and no salmon could cross that.

Engineers soon saw that they had interfered with the plans of nature; so they constructed a sloping "fish ladder" at each side of the dam. This is something like a huge staircase, about forty feet wide, with each broad step hollowed out. Water flows slowly down it, forming a wide, shallow pool in every step. The fish quickly learn to leap up one step, swim across it, and leap up to the next. They continue this until the top of the dam is reached, and then swim across the lake and on up the river.

1. To get to where they lay their eggs, salmon must _____.
   a. overcome great difficulties
   b. swim with the current
   c. find shallow rapids

2. A fish ladder is _____.
   a. a sloping river bank
   b. a series of man-made waterfalls
   c. a wide, shallow pool

3. The water falling down the fish ladder comes from _____.
   a. the Pacific Ocean
   b. a tank on top of the dam
   c. the lake created by the dam

4. How do the fish learn to climb the ladder?
   a. by being trained
   b. by trial and error
   c. by turning back

5. Each step of the ladder is probably _____.
   a. less than ten feet high
   b. about forty feet high
   c. higher than the one above it

6. Choose the best title for this story.
   a. The Columbia River
   b. A Staircase for Salmon
   c. How to Teach Fish Tricks

PERFECT SCORE: 6   YOUR SCORE: _____

This folk ballad is a story in song. (Sorry, we just have the words here: it's much better with music!) Nobody knows who sang the first ballad. Ballads were made up—and sung and enjoyed and remembered—long before they were ever written down. Singers make changes and add new things, to suit themselves. (We made some changes in this one!) This old folk song is still popular today. Maybe you've heard it. Maybe you'll sing it yourself, some day—with changes of your own.

• • •

Fox set out on a cold dark night—
  Begged the moon to give him light—
He'd many a mile to go that night,
  Before he reached the town, O!

Fox got into the Flipper-Floppers' yard,
  Where ducks and geese declared it hard
To have their rest so rudely jarred
  When the Fox was on the town, O!

He grabbed the gray goose by the neck
  And flung her over across his back.
The old duck cried out, "Quack, quack, quack!"
  And the goose's legs hung down, O!

Old Mrs. Flipper-Flopper jumped out of bed—
  Out the window popped her head—
Cried, "John, John, the gray goose is gone!
  And the Fox is on the town, O!"

John ran up to the top of the hill—
    Blew a blast both loud and shrill.
Said Fox, "That is fine music! Still,
    I'd rather not slow down, O!"

Fox hurried home to his cozy den—
    To fine little foxes . . . eight, nine, ten.
"Here's a big fat goose," he told them then,
    "Who used to live in town, O!"

Fox sat down with his hungry wife—
    Cut up the feast with fork and knife.
They never had such a supper in their life—
    And the little ones chewed on the bones, O!

1. What is this ballad mostly about?
    a. the family life of foxes
    b. a fox who went hunting
    c. a fox who lived in town

2. How did the ducks and geese feel when the fox was in the
    yard?
    a. hungry
    b. amused
    c. terrified

3. Why did John blow "a blast both loud and shrill"?
    a. He was signaling the fox that the coast was clear.
    b. He was warning other people that the fox was around.
    c. He was practicing his trumpet lesson.

4. What woke Mrs. Flipper-Flopper up?
   a. the fox barking
   b. the horn blowing
   c. the ducks and geese

5. Why was the fox out hunting?
   a. He was hungry.
   b. He loved the sound of the hunting horn.
   c. He had quarreled with his wife.

6. In this ballad, "on the town" means ———.
   a. living in town
   b. on the prowl in town
   c. out of town

7. How did the fox's family feel when he got home?
   a. disappointed
   b. puzzled
   c. happy

8. After supper, the fox probably ———.
   a. went hunting
   b. went to sleep
   c. stole a goose

9. Choose the best title.
   a. Fox Goes Hunting
   b. The Ballad of the Gray Goose
   c. The Little Foxes

A traveler was crossing the desert with a donkey and its driver. When they stopped for a while, the traveler rested in the donkey's shadow. He did not leave room for the driver.

"The sun is so hot!" said the driver. "Surely you can let me have just a *little* of the donkey's shade—for my head at least!"

"Certainly not," said the traveler. "Did I not hire the donkey for the whole journey?"

"Yes," said the angry driver, "you hired the donkey, all right, but not the donkey's shadow. That still belongs to me!" With these words he began to push the traveler out of the small shadow into the burning sun.

While they were so busy shouting and fighting, the donkey took to his heels and ran away. Soon he was out of sight.

The two men stopped quarreling and looked at each other, as if to say: "Now see what you've done!"

There was nothing to do but start back home. Before they had walked far, the traveler wished he had not been so greedy—especially since the driver refused to carry any of the luggage.

21

1. What had happened before the story began?
   a. The traveler and the donkey driver had quarreled.
   b. The traveler had made an arrangement with the driver.
   c. The driver had refused to hire out the donkey.

2. Probably the traveler and the driver had agreed that _____.
   a. the driver would ride the donkey
   b. the donkey would carry the luggage
   c. the donkey would ride

3. When they stopped to rest, the sun was _____.
   a. rising
   b. sinking in the west
   c. high in the sky

4. The traveler wanted _____.
   a. all of the food
   b. all of the shade
   c. enough shade for his head

5. Where was the luggage while the men were arguing?
   a. under a tree
   b. on the donkcy's back
   c. on the ground beside them

6. How did the traveler feel on the way home?
   a. regretful
   b. agreeable
   c. happy

7. What was the most important thing the traveler learned?
   a. Luggage is heavy.
   b. It is better to share.
   c. Donkeys are easily frightened.

8. Choose the best title for this story.
   a. Donkey for Hire
   b. A Sunny Day
   c. Two Friends

PERFECT SCORE: 8   YOUR SCORE: _____

Most days and nights pass quietly for cowboys when they are guarding a herd on the range. In summer the hot sun beats down fiercely on the plains, and in winter the cold wind blows the snow into drifts. Only now and then does something really exciting happen.

Late one summer night, a storm coming up over the hills frightened a herd of cattle lying quietly in the pasture. Sudden claps of thunder were answered by a roar from an old bull. Lightning flashed and rain poured down.

Suddenly the bull scrambled to his feet and started to run toward the river. The other cattle followed him. In a few moments the whole herd was running wildly.

The cowboys rode fast around the herd, trying to head off the leader. Just in time they turned the old bull away from the top of the steep river bank. In another moment the whole herd would have plunged into the water.

1. This story mainly tells _____.
   a. why cattle always follow a leader
   b. why cowboys guard a town at night
   c. how cowboys saved a herd of cattle

2. What caused the bull to run?
   a. He was frightened by the storm.
   b. He wanted to get out of the rain.
   c. He was struck by a cowboy.

3. The bull's excitement caused the rest of the herd
   to _____.
   a. stand quietly
   b. stampede
   c. sleep

4. After the excitement was over, the cowboys must have
   felt _____.
   a. relieved
   b. refreshed
   c. frightened

5. What might have happened if the leader had not been
   turned away from the river bank?
   a. The bull might have killed a cowboy.
   b. The other cattle would have scattered in every
      direction.
   c. Many cattle might have broken their legs in the fall.

6. Choose the best title for this story.
   a. The Cowboy and the Rodeo
   b. On a Cattle Ranch in Summer
   c. Hard Riding Saves the Herd

PERFECT SCORE: 6   YOUR SCORE: _____

People protect many wild animals. Do any of these animals help people—directly or indirectly?

One small animal that works mostly for our good is the beaver. Beavers are protected now, but long ago so many were trapped that they were in danger of extinction in the United States. Their highly prized skins were sent to Europe, for use in making tall hats and for trimming or making other fine clothes.

With the branches and twigs of nearby trees, beavers build dams across brooks and streams to create ponds. Then they build their lodges in the ponds, with the entrances under water.

A beaver dam helps to keep soil from washing away when heavy rains cause floods. And in times of dry weather the stored-up water in the ponds can be used by farmers to water their crops.

Beaver pools in the woods provide drinking places for deer, birds, and small wild animals. The pools also make a home for many varieties of fish. If there are enough beaver ponds in the woods, the water may even save trees from forest fires.

25

1. What is this story mainly about?
   a. how beaver dams become a nuisance
   b. why beaver dams and ponds are useful
   c. why people sometimes destroy beaver dams

2. You can tell from the story that dams built by beavers _____.
   a. provide water for many useful purposes
   b. are dangerous to other animals
   c. cause floods

3. The trapping of beavers is now _____.
   a. a popular sport
   b. a good job
   c. restricted by law

4. Which sentence below would the author most probably agree with?
   a. All animals are harmless.
   b. Beavers are fish.
   c. Beaver dams are more important than beaver hats.

5. Choose the best title for this story.
   a. The Man Who Wants to Help Animals
   b. Animals That Help Without Knowing It
   c. Doing More Harm Than Good

12

Write the missing words in the blanks.

• • •

Most dogs have a keen _____ of smell, but one
1

breed outstrips all the others. This is the bloodhound. He is

a large dog; some full-grown bloodhounds _____ as
2

much as a hundred pounds. His ears _____ long
3

and droopy and velvet-soft; his coat is usually black

_____ tan markings. Strange wrinkles running down
4

between _____ big sad eyes and along his cheeks
5

_____ him look old and wise.
6

A bloodhound must spend a year _____ the police
7

to be trained to search _____ lost persons. Now and
8

then he also tracks escaped criminals. A bloodhound

_____ follow a scent that is _____ much as
9   10

four hours old, and has been known to find a lost person

27

even after two days. The police let _____ smell some
11
piece of clothing belonging to the missing _____,
12
and they start him from the spot where the person was
last seen. The animal's sensitive _____ can
13
pick up a trail from grass the person has walked on
or bushes he has brushed against. Often bloodhounds
_____ in pairs. They work silently and very fast.
14

The world is so full of harmful bugs that we should be happy to learn of at least one helpful bug. This is the ordinary ladybug. On her small back she wears a bright orange shell dotted with little black spots. She and her friends may appear some spring morning on a windowsill in your house. When they do, gently move all these ladybugs outdoors to begin their season's work.

A ladybug's mission in life is to eat small but harmful bugs—aphids, scales, leafworms, mealybugs, and many others—and their eggs as well. The ladybug eats no flowers, leaves, vegetables, or helpful bugs. She does just what we need her to do. How is she wise enough to figure this out? No one really knows.

So useful is the ladybug to farmers and gardeners that some firms in the West offer them for sale. Bug pickers go to mountain spots where ladybugs are known to hibernate. The pickers raid the nests on the high slopes and scoop up the sleeping ladies by the thousands. Ladybugs provide natural protection for a home garden, and they are less expensive than chemical sprays.

1. What does the story tell about the ladybug?
   a. why she eats no flowers
   b. how she got her name
   c. how she is useful to people

2. Which sentence below is not directly stated in the story but seems to be true?
   a. Bug pickers collect ladybugs and sell them.
   b. Aphids, scales, leafworms, and mealybugs can ruin crops.
   c. All bugs are harmful to gardens.

3. You can tell from the story that farmers see the ladybug as _____.
   a. a friend
   b. an enemy
   c. an expensive nuisance

4. What is meant by the word "mission" as used in this story?
   a. specific task or purpose
   b. organized activity
   c. military operation

5. Ladybugs are active _____.
   a. all year round
   b. mainly in the fall and winter
   c. mainly in the spring and summer

6. Choose the best title for this story.
   a. All About Bugs
   b. New Jobs for Old Bugs
   c. Big Protection from a Small Friend

PERFECT SCORE: 6   YOUR SCORE: _____

Annie Oakley was born more than a century ago in a log cabin on a farm in Darke County, Ohio. This was still unsettled country. Farmers and their families hunted wild animals to increase the food supply. So it was not an unheard-of thing for a nine-year-old girl to pick up a rifle and go out with her older brothers and sisters to shoot wild turkeys or quail.

But Annie Oakley became a nearly perfect shot. She might have lived and died on the family farm in Ohio, completely unknown, if it had not been for this unusual talent. She was able to hit a moving target while riding a galloping horse. She could shoot the spots on a playing card tossed into the air, or knock the ashes off a cigarette held in someone's mouth. Annie did her shooting act in Buffalo Bill's Wild West Show for about twenty years, and went down in history as "Little Sure Shot."

1. This story is mainly about _____.
   a. why girls learned to shoot many years ago
   b. how a special talent made a girl famous
   c. why it is dangerous to shoot ashes from cigarettes

2. When she was nine years old, Annie helped her family by _____.
   a. taking care of the house
   b. working with the police
   c. shooting wild birds for food

3. To shoot the spots off a playing card in midair, Annie must have had _____.
   a. keen eyesight and a steady hand
   b. good riding ability
   c. a fast horse

4. Annie became famous when she used her unusual ability _____.
   a. to catch criminals
   b. to perform on the stage
   c. to shoot game

5. Which sentence is not directly stated in the story but seems to be true?
   a. Annie was an able horseback rider.
   b. Annie became a nearly perfect shot.
   c. Annie died on the family farm in Ohio, completely unknown.

6. Choose the best title for this story.
   a. Where Annie Oakley Was Born
   b. Shooting Turkeys a Hundred Years Ago
   c. Why Annie Oakley Is Remembered

PERFECT SCORE: 6   YOUR SCORE: _____

15

I noticed Red shortly after I went on duty in Alaska. To most people at the weather station, she was just another Eskimo dog belonging to the dog-sled team. But when I stooped to pat her, she sniffed my hand and face, and rolled over. We promptly became friends.

Red proved her friendship for me one cold afternoon about dusk. I was returning to the station when suddenly a huge polar bear loomed up on the path. The door was only a few feet away, but the snow was slippery and I fell, expecting the bear to land on top of me.

An instant later, I heard the growl of an Eskimo dog. Red had attacked the bear from behind! As I scrambled to my feet, Red was biting and clawing, and the angry bear was trying to shake off this wild ball of fur. The men inside the station heard the animals' howls. They came running and shot the polar bear.

1. This story is mainly about _____.
   a. a bear that saved a dog's life
   b. a man that saved a bear's life
   c. a dog that saved a man's life

2. Which word best describes how the author felt when he saw the polar bear?
   a. safe
   b. frightened
   c. courageous

3. How do you think the author felt when the dog attacked the bear?
   a. relieved, but concerned for the dog
   b. brave and ready to fight
   c. afraid of the dog

4. Which sentence below is not directly stated in the story but seems to be true?
   a. Red had attacked the bear from behind.
   b. The author is an Eskimo.
   c. The people at the weather station used dogs to help them travel.

5. How much time do you think the bear incident took?
   a. many hours
   b. a few minutes
   c. more than a day

6. Choose the best title for this story.
   a. Polar Bears in Alaska
   b. Red to the Rescue
   c. Traveling by Dog Sled

16

"It was just before Thanksgiving that we always made our apple cider," said Grandfather. "It should be called apple juice, but sixty years ago folks hereabouts always called it sweet cider. So we boys did, too.

"We used winter apples—Winesaps, Pippins, Delicious, or maybe Rome Beauties. They have the most sugar in them and the best taste. Every day after school in the autumn I helped my father pick and store the apples in our barn, and I can still remember that sweet smell!

"When it came time to make cider, my father tossed the clean apples into the small mill while I turned the crank by hand. This ground up the apples into a coarse pulp—'mash,' we called it. We put the mash into a cider press to squeeze out the juice. It drained off into a bucket, and we poured it into glass jugs. Dad always gave me the first drink of the new apple cider. M–m–m, was it good!"

1. This story is mainly about _____.
   a. what to do with leftover apples
   b. how apple cider is made in a factory today
   c. how apple cider was once made on a farm

2. Winter apples were chosen because they were the _____.
   a. biggest
   b. sweetest
   c. juiciest

3. You can tell from the first paragraph that _____.
   a. Grandfather moved across the country after he grew up
   b. Grandfather has lived in the same area since he was a child
   c. Grandfather moved from a farm to a city after he grew up

4. Which of the following statements is probably true?
   a. Winter apples are actually picked in the fall.
   b. Winter apples become ripe soon after Easter.
   c. Snow makes apples sweet.

5. You can tell from the story that Grandfather is recalling _____.
   a. a happy memory
   b. the hard work of his youth
   c. a new way to make apple cider

6. Choose the best title for this story.
   a. Making Applesauce Long Ago
   b. Visiting a Cider Mill
   c. Drinking the Winter Apples

36

In the early 1800's travel was difficult for most Americans, especially in certain parts of the country. For example, it was very hard to go by horse and wagon over narrow up-and-down trails through dense forests. At that time many people were moving west in search of cheap land. They had the problem of moving all their furniture, and their animals as well.

The flatboat solved the problem for many people. This was a large boat, made of heavy planks, with a flat bottom and square ends. There was no motor on the flatboat; there were not even sails. The boat simply drifted downstream with the current of the river. The family ate and slept in a box-like cabin that covered the middle part of the boat. The mother cooked, did the washing, and cared for the children. The father took care of the animals, which were kept at one end of the boat. He steered with a very long oar, called a sweep, which was mounted near the back end, on top of the cabin.

In this way thousands of pioneers traveled long distances down the Ohio and Mississippi rivers; and many then went farther west by wagon, over more open country.

1. This story tells _____.
   a. why the flatboat is the cheapest way to travel
   b. how the flatboat helped open up the West
   c. why the flatboat was used to fight Indians

2. Which animals were most likely to be on the flatboat?
   a. horses
   b. monkeys
   c. poodles

3. A flatboat probably looked like _____.
   a. a motor boat
   b. a big raft
   c. a steamboat

4. Land in the West in those days was _____.
   a. difficult to find
   b. not as cheap as land in the East
   c. cheaper than land in the East

5. Controlling the speed of the flatboat must have been very _____.
   a. difficult
   b. easy
   c. boring

6. Choose the best title for this story.
   a. West by Covered Wagon
   b. Downstream to the West
   c. Solving Water Problems

PERFECT SCORE: 6   YOUR SCORE: _____

Write the missing words in the blanks. The first two have been done for you.

THE EMBARRASSING EPISODE
OF LITTLE MISS MUFFET

Little Miss Muffet discovered a tuffet,

  (Which never occurred to the rest ___*of*___ us)
  ₁

And as 'twas a June day, and just about noonday,

  She wanted to eat—like the best of us.

Her diet was whey, and I hasten to ___*say*___
  ₂

  It's wholesome and people grow fat _____ it.
  ₃

The spot being lonely, the lady not only

  Discovered the tuffet, _____ sat on it.
  ₄

A rivulet grabbled beside her _____ babbled,
  ₅

  As rivulets always are thought to do,

And dragon-flies sported around and cavorted,

  As poets say dragon-flies ought to _____.
  ₆

Then, glancing aside for a moment, she spied

  A horrible sight that brought fear to her:

A hideous spider _____ sitting beside her,
  ₇

  And most unavoidably near to her!

Albeit unsightly, this creature politely

    Said: "Madam, I earnestly vow to you,

I'm penitent that I did not bring _____ hat.
                     8

    I should otherwise certainly bow _____ you."
                            9

Though anxious to please, he was so ill _____ ease
                            10

    That he lost all his sense of propriety,

And grew so inept _____ he clumsily stepped
               11

    In her plate—which is barred in Society!

This curious error completed _____ terror;
                       12

    She shuddered and growing much paler, not

Only left tuffet, but dealt him a buffet

    Which doubled _____ up in a sailor-knot.
                  13

It should be explained that at this he was pained:

    He cried: "I have vexed you, no doubt of it!

Your fist's like a truncheon." "You're still in my luncheon,"

Was all that she answered. "Get _____ of it!"
                       14

And The Moral is this: Be it madam or miss

    To whom you have something to say,

You are only absurd when you get in the curd

    But you're rude when you get in the whey!

          From Mother Goose for Grown-Ups *by Guy Wetmore Carrly*

PERFECT SCORE: 14   YOUR SCORE: _____

A car had been burglarized. The detectives didn't have much to go on—only that three men had been seen leaving the scene in an "old tan-and-white station wagon." No make, model, year, or license number. It was clearly a case for PATRIC, the new detective's helper at the Los Angeles police department.

PATRIC (for "*Pa*ttern *R*ecognition and *I*nformation *C*orrelations") is a computer system that does the same kinds of things that a detective does, but does them much faster. PATRIC is crammed full of criminal records, crime reports, information on stolen vehicles, even the favorite methods of known criminals. By instantly cross-checking bits of information fed into it, PATRIC can quickly build up more and more information, and eventually come up with likely human suspects.

In this particular case, PATRIC searched its files, and found another car crime in a different part of the city, also involving men fleeing in a tan-and-white vehicle—but this time someone had remembered part of the license number and reported it. Using this partial number, PATRIC found the names of five men who had been stopped for questioning in similar cars. The computer then searched another file on past arrests, and found that three of the five men had previously been arrested for theft from an auto! PATRIC turned over the names to the human detectives, who promptly investigated and then arrested the trio for the latest burglary.

PATRIC took 15 minutes to produce the suspects; a detective would probably have decided the case was not worth spending hours or days sifting through all that information, with the likelihood that suspects couldn't be found anyway. Even when there is more information available, the computer can save hours of detective work.

By W. David Malcolm, Jr.

1. This story is mainly about _____.
   a. the methods of known criminals
   b. how a computer cross-checks information
   c. how a computer helps detectives

2. Which sentence is a statement of opinion?
   a. The case was not worth spending hours or days on.
   b. PATRIC is crammed full of criminal records.
   c. PATRIC took fifteen minutes to produce the suspects.

3. What makes PATRIC's help so valuable to the Los Angeles police?
   a. the information the computer contains
   b. the speed and accuracy with which the computer works
   c. its ability to arrest burglars

4. Which sentence below is not directly stated in the story but seems to be true?
   a. Three men were arrested for the burglary.
   b. The witness in the case did not get very close to the getaway car.
   c. A car had been burglarized.

5. Choose the best title for this story.
   a. PATRIC
   b. Detectives at Work
   c. Super Detective

PERFECT SCORE: 5   YOUR SCORE: _____

20

In this exercise and the next one you will practice choosing the best ending for a story. Finding the best punch line for a joke is a fun way of doing this.

Read these jokes by Sonny Fox and Robert Gray. Choose the funniest punch line for each one. The Answer Page shows which punch lines were chosen by a comedian. We're not sure we always agree! And maybe you can think of even funnier ones. If so, write them down and try them out on your family and friends. See if you get a laugh.

. . .

1. The salesman's car broke down on an old country road. He lifted the car hood and looked in, when suddenly a voice behind him said, "Your problem is with the distributor."

   The salesman looked around and saw an old mule standing there. Unable to believe his ears, he said, "Did you say something?"

   "Yes," replied the mule. "Your distributor needs adjusting."

   The salesman ran to the nearest farmhouse and excitedly told the farmer about his experience.

   "Was it an old mule with a straw hat and lopsided ears?" the farmer asked.

   "Yes, yes, that's the mule I'm talking about."

   "Well, friend," the farmer replied,

   a. "That was Cousin Luke; he just *looks* like a mule."

   b. "Keep running. There's a doctor's office about a mile farther down this road."

   c. "Don't listen to a word he says. He doesn't know a thing about cars."

2. The entertainer was trying to sell his act to the agent. "My monkey is very smart," he said. "He can sing, dance, talk, and play the bongos—he is just about human."

"If he's so human," asked the agent, "why do you have him on a chain?"

"Well," replied the entertainer,

a. "I lost my watch."

b. "He owes me money."

c. "You're not looking. He has *me* on the chain."

21

These are more jokes. You choose the funniest punch lines.

•   •   •

1. The inventor rushed into the office and up to the office manager's desk. "I've done it, I've done it!" he cried. "I've invented a liquid that will dissolve anything."

   The office manager looked up, and quietly asked,

   a. "Will you drop some on the floor? I've always wanted to see China."

   b. "You think that's news? You never tried my brother's coffee."

   c. "Is that so? Then what will you put it in?"

2. Bobby went up to his father one day and challenged him to a riddle game. These were the rules: for every riddle the father missed, he had to hand his son a dollar, and for every riddle the son missed, he had to hand his father a dime.

   The son asked the first riddle: "What has seven ears, two noses, one arm, one leg, five bodies and eleven toes?"

   "I don't know," said the father, and he gave his son a dollar.

   "I don't know either," said the son—

   a. "Here's your dime."

   b. "I never was good at riddles."

   c. "It's a riddle."

Many years ago, late on a summer afternoon, a cowboy was riding across the plains of New Mexico. As he rode, he noticed a thin trail of smoke in the distance. The smoke seemed to be rising from the ground. He rode over for a closer look.

The "smoke" wasn't smoke at all, but a great swarm of bats flying out of a hole in the ground.

"Strange!" the cowboy thought. He got down off the little Appaloosa, and looked down into the hole. And that is how a great underground wonder, now called Carlsbad Caverns, was discovered.

These caverns are a series of caves and passages opening one into another. They extend for about twenty-five miles under the earth. They were probably formed about sixty million years ago, when sea water began to run over the soft limestone in this area. It dripped and trickled through cracks until it wore away the rock and hollowed out these vast underground chambers.

47

1. What is this story about?
   a. how a series of caverns was built and who built it
   b. what causes water to dissolve rocks
   c. how a series of caverns was formed and how it was found

2. Which statement below is probably true?
   a. No person had explored the cave before the cowboy found it.
   b. The cowboy got lost in the cave and never came out.
   c. There was a fire inside the cave.

3. To explore all of the chambers and passages, you would probably need to spend _____.
   a. about an hour
   b. a few days
   c. a few hours

4. Limestone is _____.
   a. found only above the ground
   b. too hard to dissolve
   c. found in New Mexico

5. The little Appaloosa was _____.
   a. a covered wagon
   b. the cowboy's horse
   c. a steep hill

6. Choose the best title for this story.
   a. Accidental Discovery
   b. Lost in a Cave
   c. More Room Underground

PERFECT SCORE: 6   YOUR SCORE: _____

Write the missing words in the blanks.

• • •

Would you like to spend all spring, _____, and fall
₁
just getting ready to sleep all winter? That's what the fat,
lazy woodchuck does. "Spring housecleaning" means
pushing the old dirt from the floors of the den out the front
door, getting _____ of old unused food stored in the
₂
tunnels, and perhaps enlarging the quarters _____
₃
adding a room or two.

Summertime is the ideal _____ for eating. It is
₄
then that grass, clover, flowers, and vegetables _____
₅
richest and sweetest. During mid-morning a woodchuck
stuffs himself _____ food. Then he has a nap
₆
_____ the shade. Before dark he has _____
₇   ₈
another big meal. Comfortably full, the woodchuck crawls
_____ his den for the night.
₉

With all this resting and eating he gets very _____,
10
of course. By fall he _____ barely move enough to
11
carry a little green food into his storehouse for the
_____. Once this is done, _____ calls several
12   13
of his friends together and they plug up the "doors" to the
den and begin their long winter's _____.
14

24

Here are some actual quotes from accident reports submitted to insurance companies by unlucky drivers. Read them and see if you can decide why each one is funny and whether you understand what the writer really meant.

There are no questions to answer. But it will be fun to see if you agree with other people in your class and to talk about the various cases.

Try not to laugh too hard till it's time to talk!

•   •   •

1. Coming home, I drove into the wrong house and collided with a tree I don't have.

2. The other car collided with mine without giving warning of its intentions.

3. I thought my window was down, but found it was up when I put my hand through it.

4. I collided with a stationary truck coming the other way.

5. The guy was all over the road; I had to swerve a number of times before I hit him.

6. I pulled away from the side of the road, glanced at my mother-in-law, and headed over the embankment.

7. I had been driving for forty years when I fell asleep at the wheel and had the accident.

8. An invisible car came out of nowhere, struck my vehicle, and vanished.

9. I was thrown from my car as it left the road. I was later found in a ditch by some stray cows.

10. The telephone pole was approaching. I was attempting to swerve out of its way when it struck my front end.

11. I was unable to stop in time and my car crashed into the other vehicle. The driver and passengers then left immediately for vacation with injuries.

Answer Page

Answer Page
Read Beyond the Lines, Book C

Exercise Number	Question 1	Question 2	Question 3	Question 4	Question 5	Question 6	Question 7
1	c	b	b	c	a	c	
2	b	a	c	b	b	c	
3	c	c	a	b	c .	b	
4	c	a	b	c	a	c	b
5	b	a	c	b	c	b	
6	lucky	how	school	taught	station	he	train
7	a	b	c	b	a	b	
8	b	c	b	c	a	b	c
9	b	b	c	b	c	a	b
10	c	a	b	a	c	c	
11	b	a	c	c	b		
12	sense	weigh	are	with	his	make	with
13	c	b	a	a	c	c	
14	b	c	a	b	a	c	
15	c	b	a	c	b	b	
16	c	b	b	a	a	c	
17	b	a	b	c	a	b	
18	of	say	on	but	and	do	was
19	c	a	b	b	c		
20	c	c					
21	c	a					
22	c	a	b	c	b	a	
23	summer	rid	by	time	are	with	in
24							

Question 8	Question 9	Question 10	Question 11	Question 12	Question 13	Question 14	Exercise Number
							1
							2
							3
							4
							5
in	them	was	to	give	be	over	6
							7
b	a						8
a							9
							10
							11
for	can	as	him	person	nose	work	12
							13
							14
							15
							16
							17
my	to	at	that	her	him	out	18
							19
							20
							21
							22
eaten	into	fat	can	winter	he	sleep	23
							24

Progress Chart

Progress Chart
Read Beyond the Lines, Book C

After each exercise number, color the boxes to show how many
questions you answered correctly. For example, if you get four
questions right in exercise 1, color the first four boxes.

MY SCORE   Name: _____

Exercise Number	1	2	3	4	5	6	7
1							░
2							░
3							░
4							
5							░
6							
7							░
8							
9							
10							░
11						░	
12							
13							░
14							░
15							░
16							░
17							░
18							
19						░	░
20			░	░	░	░	░
21			░	░	░	░	░
22							░
23							
24	░	░	░	░	░	░	░

8	9	10	11	12	13	14	Exercise Number
▓	▓	▓	▓	▓	▓	▓	1
▓	▓	▓	▓	▓	▓	▓	2
▓	▓	▓	▓	▓	▓	▓	3
▓	▓	▓	▓	▓	▓	▓	4
▓	▓	▓	▓	▓	▓	▓	5
							6
▓	▓	▓	▓	▓	▓	▓	7
		▓	▓	▓	▓	▓	8
	▓	▓	▓	▓	▓	▓	9
▓	▓	▓	▓	▓	▓	▓	10
▓	▓	▓	▓	▓	▓	▓	11
							12
▓	▓	▓	▓	▓	▓	▓	13
▓	▓	▓	▓	▓	▓	▓	14
▓	▓	▓	▓	▓	▓	▓	15
▓	▓	▓	▓	▓	▓	▓	16
▓	▓	▓	▓	▓	▓	▓	17
							18
▓	▓	▓	▓	▓	▓	▓	19
▓	▓	▓	▓	▓	▓	▓	20
▓	▓	▓	▓	▓	▓	▓	21
▓	▓	▓	▓	▓	▓	▓	22
							23
▓	▓	▓	▓	▓	▓	▓	24

This is to certify that

_____
Student

has successfully completed
READ BEYOND THE LINES, Book C,
and is deserving of the commendation
that this award represents.

_____
Teacher